Whispers & Musings: Beneath Midnight Stars & Mountain Peaks

My poetic tales through times and emotions

Hari

BookLeaf Publishing
India | USA | UK

Made with ❤ on the BookLeaf Publishing Platform
www.bookleafpub.in
www.bookleafpub.com

To the peerless poets,

To the divine, the eternal author.

To my soul, forever attuned to divine echoes.

To the whisperers of the wind and the voices among the stars.

This collection is dedicated to the silent tales

And ageless wisdom that illuminate my lyrical journey.

Acknowledgement

My heartfelt gratitude to God, my teachers, my family, and my friends, as well as to the many inspiring souls who have touched my life. To those whose insights, emotional responses, and wisdom have shaped my poetic journey; to the silent wonders of nature; and to all that is beautiful and glorious—thank you for being my muse.

I extend my deepest appreciation to BookLeaf Publishing for their unwavering support in bringing this collection to life. Your guidance has been invaluable.

Lastly, to the readers who join me on this journey—your presence is the greatest gift. May these poems find a home in your heart, inspiring you to see the world through a lens of wonder and beauty.

Preface

As I embark on this poetic journey, I am drawn to the timeless beauty that resides within the simplest moments of life. Through this collection, Whispers & Musings: Beneath Midnight Stars & Mountain Peaks, I have sought to capture the splendor of nature, the depth of human emotion, and our shared, eternal quest for meaning. Each poem reflects not only my quiet conversations with the world but also the universal wisdom that unites us all.

From the soft whispers of the natural world to the profound stirrings of the human heart, my hope is that these poems resonate with you, awakening a deeper connection to both the everyday and the extraordinary. Thank you for being a part of this journey. May these verses bring you solace, joy, and a renewed sense of wonder.

Genre I:
Salutation & Tribute

Ode to the Divine Poet

Salutations to the one who gave us the sun and moon,
And gratitude for the starry night sky that sparkles through the gloom!
Salutations to the one who weilds all the forces of nature,
And gratitude for the hills and dales, narrating countless tales of stature.

Salutations to the one whose creation is an endless poem—
The master of verse and rhyme, to Him, I dedicate all my whispered lines!
May the glorious one breathe life into my lyrical song!

Those whispers and silent tales drawn deep,
where they belong.

May those silent tales rise as whispers on the wind,
Carrying ageless wisdom, timeless poetry beneath the midnight stars!
May my songs dissolve in air and flow through water,
Bringing forth life's glory, love, and all that the heart holds dear!

Million Poetical Dreams

Like weaving imaginations to create designs,
Poetry is more than just a rhyme of words.
My feelings, refined, clothed in metrics' grace,
I set them free to flow through varied tunes.

Like the warm rays of the rising sun,
My gentle poem begins and gathers greater strength.
Like the soothing phases of the glowing moon,
My quiet voice swells as the poem grows in length.

Like the sparkling beauty of the dark night
skies,
My poetry shines with its luminous highs.
Standing tall and still, like rooted trees,
These verses of hope are planted in hearts'
dreams.

The birds of the sky are awake, taking flight,
My words flutter like wings in the bright
sunlight.
The creatures of lakes chase their rippling
wakes,
These verses propel like fins beneath the
waves.

Poets, do they ever craft poems?
Poems like mothers, bear many poets.
If poets write, they are poetic attempts.
If poems arise, they reveal lovely mysteries,
Only in such verses sprout a million poetical
dreams.

O Savior Delight!

I bow to You,
the eternal refuge of all,
Who in essence
is one and all.
Your pure intelligence
remains universal;
before You, none great
and no one small!

The all-pervading,
attributeless One—
the one worthy
of all adoration.
This universe,
mere appearance,
You, its cause—
beyond mere apparition.

The only Creator,
Preserver, and Destroyer—
Mother, sweeter; Father, nourisher;
And dreadful terror.
Giver of law, wealth,
and tender passions,
the dispenser Lord
of fruits of human achievements.

You're immutable
as supreme spirit,
Who is neither
this nor even that.
Refuge of all beings
in the wilderness lost,
Redeemer of all beasts
with an impure past.

Bigger than biggest
of all that exists,
smaller than an atom
that here persists.
More stable among
the changing subsists,
noblest of all
noble pursuits.

Truth, essence,
and eternal light—
save us all
from our folly's flight.
Friend of all,
O Savior, delight!
Goal of all beings
by simple birthright!

In You, in You alone,
may we rest.
On You, on You alone,
may we invest.
Only You, only You alone,
may we lovest.
In You, in You alone,
we ever trust!

Noblest of all
noble pursuits,
Friend of all,
O Savior, delight!
In essence,
You alone are best—
None made lower;
You are the greatest!

Genre II:
Spiritual Reflections

Dream not, sleep not

Let sleep go to sleep; dreams are truths asleep.
For those awake—are only dreaming long!
No dreams come true; all are mere illusions.
The Upanishads clarion call out aloud.

Turiya, the fourth, alone is real.
Neither ocean nor waves remain true—vast or small.
Reality bestows truth on all dreams, asleep or awake.
For those awake—are only dreaming long!

For the awakened heart, Self alone is true.
What matters if Truth stays unseen?
Dream, sleep, wakefulness—three veils of Self unknown.
For those awake—are only dreaming long!

For the longing heart, truth always draws near.
March on, march on; stop not your stride.
Arise, awake, journey ever onward.
For those awake—are only dreaming long!

Dream not, sleep not; illusions melt like mist.
For those awake—are only dreaming long!
Self is so near, the soul unbound.
Go beyond, go beyond; illusions won't rebound.

Quest for Meaning

The calm seas, the silent waves;
A ship with wings that carries men;
All I hear is mental chatter on—
Rumble, rumble, noise within;

White and grey streaks on canvas blue;
Hands unseen of the painter unknown;
Patterns sketched from unseen brush strokes;
Drawn and erased at an insane pace!

Are these floating froths remnants from the past?
Are they the jars of ink that remain unused?
I seek to know its creator, if there's one.
What created it and from whence it came?

Even the mightiest forces lie subdued,
When inner turbulence remains unexpressed.
In this transformation, I'm unperturbed,
Stormy weather or gentle breeze, stay
undisturbed.

Like rogues unleashed upon the helpless,
This mighty force leaves countless losses.
Grim and gloomy, pale with despair,
A nasty dance that leaves trails of gore.

Then the brush that paints this sky,
Paints nothing but a ravaging pain.
Its truth revealed in the passage of time,
When it starts to rain, it never restrains.

Deeper sighs, unsteady breaths;
Like the storms that hit the skies,
Recur ever, having no shame or shyness.
Profound questions in my mind arise.

How high might I soar from here?
My sights remain on the ground below.
What the hell do I have on this earth?
When no heavens are seen up in clouds above!

In my try to rise above so high,
With my sights firmly settled low,
Should I climb up or seek to fly?
When my focus is tethered below.

On what does it rest, yet never rests?
On whom does it depend, yet independent?
What could bind that remains ever free?
If the sky falls, on what does it ever befall?

Is it vapor, smoke, or dust, all the same?
Heavenly prism that splits no light at all.
White and bright, blue and lit overall,
Great or small, don't they float above all?

Mysteries Revealed

The calm seas and the silent waves;
In the ship of pursuit, I make my moves;
Always I attempt to stay silent—
Rumble not and grumble not.

All I seek is to calm my mind,
The passing thoughts like clouds unbound.
A quest in earnest as my search begins;
Be the witness like the sky to clouds.

Sky to clouds is localized,
While the cosmic expanse is universalized.
Where sounds and noises in rumbling might,
Only in pure silence, truth is caught.

White and grey streaks on canvas blue;
More colors are added too.
Black or blue, grey or white,
The seer alone does illuminate.

The floating fragments from remnants past,
The jars of ink do not go to waste.
Endless paintings in silence vast,
Like rivers in motion, they reach oceans fast.

All those thoughts came from the past,
Rising and falling in grasping haunt.
Scenes upon scenes, they bother me not.
Past or future, in conflict I am uncaught.

When the mightiest force has been subdued,
No turbulence remains to be expressed.
In this transformation, I'm unperturbed,
Stormy weather or gentle breeze, stay
undisturbed.

Rogues, lost in extreme cluelessness,
No force is mighty, none counts the loss.
Despair is gone, and gloom dispersed.
This elegant dance, my heart relished.

The calm seas, the silent waves;
Moves swift within a placeless place,
Silent sounds it propagates,
Deeper into the spaceless space.

None to paint and nothing to paint,
Who can paint with a no-paint?
Where there's no time or clime, what art
remains?
Limitless, I am without constraints.

Questions merged where answers arise.
Quest and thirst are put to rest.
Visions dissolve when wisdom rises.
Words of the wise, you can trust.

Swinging Illusions

Reality blends into illusion;
Illusion erasing reality.
Reality is no imagination—
On careful examination.

Truth reflects:

A mirror that reflects—
In broad daylight.
The just are punished
When vision distorts,
And illusion snares.

Reality blends into illusion;
Illusion dissolves reality.

Worst is not the best:

Glitter that shines—
In shady lights.
Fools appear great,
But nearer one goes,
The true mother of pearls shows.

Reality is no imagination—
On careful examination.

Fears gather fuel:

Shadows that dance—
On crescent nights.
Lies masquerade as Truth;
Rumors never stop,
Under shadowy rules.

Reality lost in illusion;
Illusion veiling reality.

Mere distortion marvels:

Wavy vapors flow—
On distant sights.
Reality's fabric unravels,
And none remains
The further one moves.

Reality is a true vision—
On vigilant inspection.

Truth shines as is:

The snake that moves—
In dusky twilight.
Perception ever misleads;
The fear that grips
Goes when rope emerges.

Reality mocks illusion;
Illusion distracts realism.

Dangers in dark prevail:

A ghost appears—
On dim-lit nights.
Imaginations quickly fade;
Faintly heart palpitates,
Slows when a pole appears.

Reality destroys imagination—
On alert observation.

Flimsy unrealities:

Windy whistles whisper—
Sound of rustling leaves.
Rumors hide some secrets;
Falsehoods stop
Where truth reveals.

Reality dispels illusion;
Illusion tricks the right vision.

Life's bitter experiences:

A flamed torch flickers—
When fuel depletes.
With age, wisdom grows;
The passion dies
When reason guides.

Reality blends into illusion;
Illusion dissolves reality.

Reality is no imagination—
On careful examination.

And so it remains—
Illusion in darkness shines.
Close to the edge of truth,
Life swings back and forth.

Solitude by the Shore

A lonely island, I, the sole witness stand.
Sun on a lazy morning, I sat on the dew-kissed sand.
The waves caress the shoreline, a soothing serenade,
As I sit, lost in thought, on this peaceful coastal beachside.

As the morning light ascends, the world quietly awakens,
Seagulls soar above, their cries, a melancholic cadence.
I breathe the salty air, feeling the ocean's gentle might,
A sense of calm washes over me, in this solitary delight.

Time stands still, as I gaze out at the endless
blue,
My heart, a reflection of the sea, with depths
anew.
In this quiet moment, I find solace and peace,
A sense of belonging to the universe, my
soul's release.

Echoes of my Soul

A million questions swirl, moment to moment I sway.
My will, weakened, and my hope lost day by day.
Yet, memories submerged, like anchors, hold me fast.
Shadows of sorrow, fetters that bind, forever to last.

But then, rays of hope appear, like oars in sight.
I grasp them tight, and climb aboard, to brave the dark of night.

I search for a life with oceanic might,
Where the tides of time, and the depths of
sorrow lose their fight.

All that's green, I know, is never permanent,
it's true,
But still, I'll hold on to hope, and wish to see
this journey through.
Where momentary joys turn into a steadying
wind,
To unfurl the mast and to reach the shores
safe and sound.

Genre III:
Nature and Seasons

Morning's Veil

The world drifts between sleep and awake,
The sun in the sky takes its time to wake.
The darkness, reluctant to give its stake,
I glimpsed a large diamond lake.

The object near, both real and surreal,
A blanket spread on a grassy isle.
With eager delight, my heart did fill—
In curiosity, I touched the flakes so chill.

Many balls of cotton, drops of diamonds,
Soft and frothy, or so it seems,
Glowing, snowy, and flaky dreams,
Arcs of light on leafy greens.

Like a million fairies, they spoke in light.
A feast for the eyes, a magical sight,
Gentle droplets bringing pure delight,
Nature's child on a midnight flight,
Whispering truths of life's transient plight.

String of pearls of shimmering kind,
Moisture drops in their soft unwind.
In colder months, a treasure find,
Grassy patches where this dew reclined,
Our early hours feel well refined.

When the lord of the sky begins to shine,
The darkness no longer claims its reign.
The diamond balls take flight, then wane,
Leaving no trace, they'll come back again.
For lingering here holds no lasting gain.

Gentle dew, gentle dew, where have you
flown?
Up in the air, as vapor, you've grown.
To a world where you're not to be seen,
To repeat your delicate dance, serene, unseen.

Sunrise Symphony

The darkness veil lifted, no longer enshrouded,
As heaven's lamp lit the horizon, proudly vowed.
Swift appearance of the first radiant light,
This illuminating sight, a wonder delight.

The melodious birds attuned to the breeze,
Echoing the musical notes with tranquil ease.
Nature, the captivated audience, in full attendance,
The sun god's orchestra creating harmonious dance.

The glow, feeble to bright, the scene unfolded wide,
As morning's silence stirred life inside.
All creation stood in reverent stillness,
Under the morning sun's soft, golden brilliance.

The rest now get a chance to rest,
As the rest of the world in motion set.
The colors and hues are all well reset,
As the blazing sun started rising in the East.

The Sunset Blaze

The vibrant orange hue of the setting sun,
Painted the horizon with a gentle blush,
undone.
A fleeting moment where day and night
reside,
A peaceful sight where heart and soul abide.

Soft orange embers of the setting sun,
Grace the horizon, a breathtaking sight
begun.
A moment to behold, in tranquil hue,
Day bids farewell, in vibrant colors, anew.

Moons of seasons

The awakening spring moon,
Gardens full of blossoms adorn.
Spring breezes carry flowery fragrant;
Having an intoxicating sweet scent.

The bright pink summer moon,
Relief from scorching summer sun.
Nature fills poets with fiery passion,
And inspires poetic expression.

The moon hides in the monsoon,
Where rain alone takes its reign.
Mixture of disdain and soothing,
When cuckoos' songs are air-filling.

The full and brighter autumnal moon,
Trees don full of leaves golden.
Symphony of sounds from rustling;
Lighting the Earth from falling.

Then comes calling of the cold moon,
With skies changing colors soon.
With early winter flowers in bloom,
As the bees and birds escape gloom.

Come, come, Winter's long, chill moon,
Your biting cold won't leave us soon.
Sweaters and mufflers give us protection,
Joys and sorrows vying for an equation.

As seasons turn, the moons remain,
A constant presence, a cyclical refrain.

Moon, the wonder

Moon is nature's great magic spell.
A shining wonder with a touch of tragic tale to tell,
Stories of waxing and waning straight,
From folklores across cultures, speaking bright.

The moon is nature's unique creation.
A no-moon night is called a new moon's formation.
In phases dark and bright, it reveals its face,
A planetary dance in a celestial pace.

The moon is humankind's fascination,
Poets and scientists hold it in admiration.
Many religious rituals find their synchronization,
Adoring giants in joyful celebration.

The moon is humankind's fascination,
With astrologers and astronomers in
exploration,
For the latter, a small step is a giant leap;
For the former, destiny's fruits are reaped in
time.

The moon is unique in many ways.
Shining with pure white, silvery rays,
Drawing its power from the Sun's warm light,
Its power to eclipse is an astronomer's delight.

The moon indeed has many shapes to share.
Waxing and waning in gibbous, crescent care,
Left and right, its phases unfold,
A constant change, forever to behold.

In the lunar cycle, we find our place,
Connected to the moon's gentle, growing
phase.
A magical wonder, a true source of light,
The moon, a constant companion through
the night.

Whispers of Starry Night Sky

A great, infinite expanse so wide,
A vast canvas stretching on every side,
A million diamonds scattered, cosmic pride,
Twinkling lights in their celestial ride.

In the swirling Milky Way above the sky,
A billion lamps shine to the naked eye,
Inspiring kids and elders forever, both alike,
Like sparkling angels, igniting interests to
spike.

Clusters of stars form zodiac signs,
The sun takes its fixed celestial positions,
Deciding calendar months in endless cycles spun,
A cosmic rhythm repeats its run.

Stars hold secrets on a cosmic scale,
From dust, new worlds are born in a celestial tale,
Galaxies spiral, elliptical, or collide,
A dance delight, massive, celestial, and wide.

Birthing many mythological tales and stories,
From different cultures, revealing mysteries,
Fabricating science and myth in equal beauties,
Weaving a web of million magical spells.

The magic spells told in secret whispers,
To bright, sparkling kids through bedtime stories,
And fairy tales on silent nights, for ages retold,
Bringing streaming dreams from afar, in wonder to behold.

Invigorating Spring

Nature's Symphony.
Among the seasons, its name resounds.
Life shoots forth with fresh, new grounds.
Tender blooms, joy-sustaining,
Thrills of newness, well affirming.

Blooming Joy.
Of verdant shoots and freshly blooms,
A promise in nature, life resumes.
Happiness winds freely blowing.
Nature's whispers, gently soothing.

Artful Coloring.
The radiant hues in spring, cheers.
The flowers open, nectar invites bees.
Dew's touch, a precious blessing.
Sun's kiss, a divine caressing.

Season's Seasoning.
All fragrant scents, a joyful dance,
Chorus of perfumes in deeper trance.
Aromatic smells self-emanating,
Unleash subtle honey flavoring.

Renewed Vibrancy.
Newborns feel a pure delight.
Newer life kindle magic light.
A lovely paradise, love-quenching,
Brings new fruits, sweetly bursting.

No Humdrum.
Life's moments, truly pulsating,
Hummingbirds arrive, honey suckling.
Vibrant wings pulse, softly drumming,
Bees and creatures sing, unending.

Majestic Splendor Reigns.
Spring's arrival, life claims its crown;
Majestic blooms, their beauties shown.
O Spring, our king, keeps reigning,
Spring, indeed, the most invigorating!

Autumnal Blooms: Wisdom Springs, Death Teaches

The autumn blooms amidst summer and winter,
Creating a serene atmosphere.
A range of trees, plants, and shrubs
Surrender their leaves and blooms.

Rustling noises, melodious notes,
Fluttering leaves playing instruments.
Rusty, brownish, burgundy fall is nice and earthy,
Smoother, softer, crispier vibrates all musically.

This season is the art of dying gently,
Inviting a new generation freshly.
The acts of fall remain praiseworthy,
Its graceful exit, truly noteworthy.

As fall descends, no one falls,
Revealing truths, an act not false.
Leaving memories of past creations,
Nurturing hope and fresh aspirations.

The past is gone when autumn's shed,
Live in the present to remain unafraid.
After death, the cold will creep,
A message clear for us to keep.

Deciduous trees in forests show,
Following cycles that ebb and flow.
Like in penance, trees consume less,
Feeling indoors while still outdoors.

Fall imparts great wisdom,
Nature doesn't suffer boredom.
What spring brings, autumn sheds,
Death and birth, not surreal truths.

The Majestic Monsoon King's Journey

Signs of Arrival

The long, sunny days, with temperatures soaring high,
End the parched land's wait, once barren and dry.
Eager visitors from the seas draw near,
Bringing their gifts, our welcomed guests appear.

Welcoming the First Touch

Before the king arrives, the drums in retinue beat,
Before the monsoon comes, the petrichor scents greet.

Worshipping the mother's right foot in the
west,
Washing with sacred waters, raising the land
to rest.

Drenching the Land

The monsoon winds rise, to the knees and
past the waist,
Drenching and flooding the coastal lands in
haste.
Filling the lakes, swelling the rivers, taking no
rest,
Flowing through the nestled hills of the
Deccan's crest.

Reaching the Himalayan Countries

As the stream of winds unrest, June gives way
to August,
Heavenly clouds prepare to caress the land's
breast.
The driest parts now breathe through a cooler
chest,

Gradually touching the foothills of the
Himalayas with zest.

A Parallel Arm Towards Bengal

The king's retinue takes a parallel path,
Flowing through emerald lands, a drop
beneath.
Taking a long curve toward Bengal, it waits—
For the king's return through Himalayan
gates.

Retreating Season

In his beating retreat, the victor conquers the
lands left,
On eastern shores and through the heart,
with great spirit.
October and November, carry his
diminishing trait,
Returning to the great oceanic home, royal
retreat.

Monsoon Strikes

Nature dances, pure delight,
The season's transience, absolute plight.
To end the summer's blazing bright,
Arrives the monsoon in its thunderous might.

Deluges swell the lakes and streams,
Breaching banks, surging to extremes.
Through valleys low and peaks so high,
The monsoon bursts—goodbye, dry sky.

The Symphony of Rains

The orchestra of winds,
Clouds thunder with their drums,
Trees strumming their strings—
Nature's music softly hums.

The rhythmic song the cuckoo sings,
Egrets and herons compose their notes,
Peacocks perform their radiant dance,
While other birds weave melodious tropes.

Toads and frogs croak in cheer,
Snails and crabs migrate afar.
Snakes and turtles lay their eggs in place,
Reptiles rest in tranquil grace.

Ants retreat to their safe burrows,
Alates dance with mates in a show.
Termites lay their eggs in grooves—
The insect life cycle is in flow.

Dragonflies and butterflies
Join in the new musical bands.
Deer and langurs in their trances,
Beetles seek their moonlit romances.

Monsoon's Delight

The scent of wet earth awakes,
Like a child cradled in a mother's embrace.
With petrichor's effervescent secrets,
The land is rebirths in a tender mess.

The skies are painted with hues
Of dark blue and purple views,
As clouds congregate and clash,
Their soft murmurs echo like symphonic
trumpets.

The wind carries the whispers
Of a thousand gentle giant fingers,
Dancing across the vast expanse—
The land is blessed with an artful grace.

The monsoon applies a kind
Cooling balm on parched land,
Quenching thirst and soothing souls,
As the land awakens and shines with new
goals.

Genre IV: Love and Romance

A Heart's Plea

Spare a moment for a man of heart,
One that bleeds not blood, but love from the start.
Spare a moment, if you can,
For when love bleeds, it shatters a million hearts with prickly pain.

Spare a moment, O readers of poetry,
Not for beauty's sake, but for my love's at stake, losing all harmony.
Spare a moment, if you can,
Not for a sympathy show, but to carry my love to her heart's span.

Spare a moment, my dear readers, to see
Molecules of my love manifesting into pain or ecstasy.
Spare a moment, if only you can,
For all hearts speak in a tongue universal, and beat as one, as a loving clan.

Yet, spare another moment to behold,
How love's darkest nights give way to light, two hearts to enfold.
For in the end, let not my love become a curse,
But two hearts found, in love's embrace, sweet success.

Spare your moments, O all things she loves and holds true,
In my despair, I reach out to you.
Borrow my love, return it to her heart,
For I am lost without her love, and we're torn apart.

Spare a thought, O all things that bring her joy,
In my darkness, I reach out to you with a ploy,
Borrow my love, and return it to her heart,
To find a place in her bosom and never be lost.

Love's Timeless Grip

In mid-August's warmth, when our eyes first met,
A fleeting glance, yet countless eons were reset.
A strange, unseen force bound me with threads of fate,
Sealing my heart with a feeling unknown and strange beset.

You occupied my thoughts, breaths, and dreams,
Since that fateful day, as far as my memory summons.
Days and nights went past, and all my sleeps were lost,
Unaware if defeat was waiting, ready to hurt.

Not knowing what, why, or how it all
happened,
After two complete months, when all of it
dawned,
For me to have known, I was lost in love at
first glance.
I was merely lost in the wilderness of a solo
romance.

It must have been deep, like the dark blue
pond.
Even my mental message, you didn't miss.
Within a few moments' past, more details you
asked.
Glad was I, a lengthy write-up I shared.

I thanked the Cosmos that carried my
whispers,
That reached only your tender inner ears.
A few such times, the magic had worked,
Until the time when cool November arrived.

On a moonlit night, I shared something more.
You sent a reply, a mystery I could never
forget.
Since that night, only your gentle name I
hear,
Echoing from the depths of my heart,
through every pore.

Fairy Blue Light of Love in Sight

Mysterious Signs of Love Revealed

Once upon a time, on a night stroll beneath star-studded skies,
A radiant, ethereal glow suddenly caught me by surprise.
Magically appearing as a shimmering, blue-hued rod of light,
It swiftly moved past, just above my shoulder height.

In a fleeting moment, before it vanished from sight,
A message from her on my gadget opened up straight.
Revealing a hidden secret in an unexpected moment,
It connected my heart to a lively, mystical thread.

All shades of blue, her heart's hue, a mysterious cosmic sign,
A coincidence that left me wonder-struck: Do our stars align?
From where the glow appeared and where it disappeared from view,
I know not; I only pursue the universe's subtle weave.

A series of events showed fate's intricate design,
For two months, a mystical bind held me in its sway, so divine.

She, my fairy princess, migrated into my heart,
Forever living, moving in and out, like a well-kept secret art.

I tried to keep my mental balance, a delicate inner dance,
A magical, unspoken bond, like a treasure to enhance.
Thus, a year passed with my situation in unease;
To tell her or not was disturbing my mental peace.

All attempts to hide it manifested strange suffering;
I awaited a natural moment to show my feelings.
At last, one day, the wait was over,
And I plunged into a sequence complicated forever!

Plunging into The Sacred Unknown Path

The poignant moments of unrequited love,
The overpowering feelings that she remains unaware behove .
My falling in love or admiration was never planned;
My mysterious experiences rooted deeply, strongly bound.

The beautiful and deep contrasts we share,
Her thoughtful self-love, my feelings I bear.
The indelible marks my heart still withholds,
In deeper depths of sacred space, it eternally beholds.

Unmindful of feelings unreturned or lost in the cosmos,
I remain vulnerable in perpetually colorful dramas.

Victory of Love

In moments shared, your words linger in the air,
A hint about wine, a jest, a playful dare.
You, my hidden nectarine, a sweet refrain—
What greater pleasure could another feign?

"Dare beyond fear lies victory," you said;
In truths unspoken, hearts may forge ahead.
If true, then to you, these words I confide:
Will you, my love, forever walk by my side?

"What?" you replied, a moment's surprise;
Yet unspoken truths still dance in my eyes.
Let silence speak where words hesitate to tread;
In quiet glances, my hopes softly thread.

And once you whispered, "Moh Maya" in a jovial jest,
I smiled, for I knew the truth inside best.
I replied, if it was an infatuation, I wouldn't trust,
This is something more, and I let my heart celebrate.

You, my hidden nectarine, again I ask—
My only love, will you—by my side—forever walk?
To revel in the truth where our hearts forge ahead,
In a glimmering hope, my days softly tread.

The Symphony of Longing

My lovely love, a melodious symphony plays within,
With the harmony of beats, waiting for my love to begin.
My lovely love, nectarine-sweet music flowing within,
With dripping honey drops, waiting for my love to win.

My lovely love, a wine made of mystery-filled dopamine,
With stimulating euphoria, waiting to drown me in.

My lovely love, a musth of elephants that
madly run,
In a mad sensation, I am waiting to be
overrun.

My lovely love, a trail of scent, pheromones so
fine,
Subtly sprinkled to weave an amorous play
divine.
My lovely love, my vibrant feathers are open
wide,
In a courtship dance, with bright plumage, I'll
be gently mild.

My lovely love, you're arrows made of flowers.
Shot towards me by Cupid, god of love's
showers.
My lovely love, you're in my deepest of
longings.
Now, my sense and shame has become lost
belongings.

Embrace in Dreams

Only dreams are made of dreamy stuff!
Some dreary, others fairy, dreams bear
Sweeter dreams when my sweetheart is
nearer,
Once I found her lost in deepest fear,
With my longing heart, I slowly drew near.

My gentle touch— warm, and her tears
warmer.
Her tresses disheveled, she— my sweetheart
charmer.
What passed between our hearts, our embrace
exchanged.
On my careful touch, her expressions slightly
changed.

As my fingers caressed her dishevelled tresses,
Guiding her strands into gentle, smooth
presses.
As the lids of her eyes closed softly aloft,
The pains of her heart waned quite a lot.

We stood there to the sound of barking dogs,
Hearing the eerie noise from rustling trees
across.
As the gentle breeze began to caress us,
Our senses caught the fragrant scent of roses.

Was it a sunny day or starry night? I know
not,
Deeply drowned in thoughts, we are caught.
Streaming tears down her cheeks, my heart
collects,
Bathing my soul truly in a noble purpose.

As we stood together in timeless silence,
Only letting her tears speak in eloquence.
My witnessing heart touching her pendant,
I stayed true to my resolute commitment.

When no spoken words were exchanged,
And no hands of time could be contained,
When our senses caught the emotional
strains,
What need for any language still remains?

In our warm embrace, time stood stilled,
Only silence spoke, our hearts felt swelled.
With her cheek on my chest for solace,
And my brow on hers in tight embrace.

Where moments passed as if they were eons,
And eons, like they were fleeting moments.
Time and age simply lost all their sense,
The lasting meaning was from our very
presence.

In an unsplit fraction, my dear moved away.
With the scene gone, is when dreams betray,
Leaving those moments never ever to sway.
Memories made stuff sweeter ever to stay.
Only dreams can be made from dreamy stuff!

True Love Endures

In quiet hours,
your presence fills my mind.
In a shadowed path,
am I entwined?

You, with your love
for verse in every tongue,
And to the nectar from vines,
your passions are strung.

Honest and bold—
your words like a whispering breeze.
Your heart's secrets to me
remain in veiled unease.

Books and plays—
your worlds within your grasp.
A universe apart,
you're a soul to clasp.

What drew my heart close
can't be defined.
Yet your essence, pure,
a treasure, refined.

Unspoken are my feelings
as they softly start.
For you, my heart beats,
quietly apart.

Like the fledgling creeper
needing support,
My lovely feelings
yearned for your rapport.

A strong wind
shakes the creeper's grasp.
Unseen forces
drew my yearnings to collapse.

Like the matured plants,
often cut back,
Springs forth
its shoots in multi-stack.

The more you pruned my feelings
and cut them back,
In numerous ways
they were back on track.

You, with your love for verse
in every tongue,
Will I ever captivate you
with this song sung?

Books and plays—
your worlds within your grasp.
Will my books too play
in your tight clasp?

To love—
is it a sin, unpardonable?
To long and hope—
are they regrettable?

Very long
has been my longing.
Longer my hope—
my heart still ringing.

I might be long gone,
but my words are alive.
I might cease to exist;
but my love will survive.

In a shadowed path,
for I'm entwined,
The fear and fret within me
only you can unwind.

Whether quiet or not,
you're in my thoughts behind.
For no one else,
I ever entertained!

Now you know,
to me, who you are,
All my thoughts
here laid threadbare.

Trials strong
as a headwind,
What weathers the storm
alone stays behind.

True is my love—
when will you find?
To keep us close—
forever in this eternal bind!

Seasons of Longing

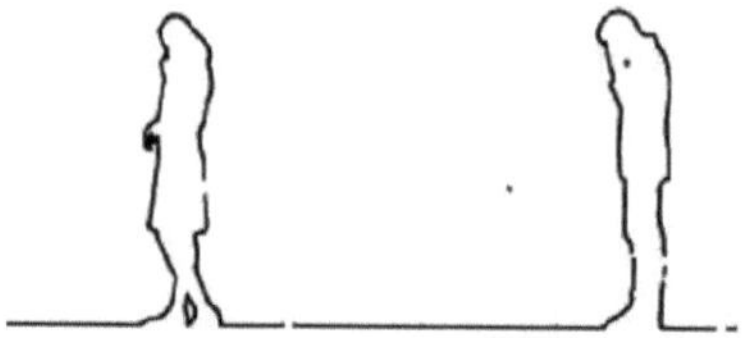

Of the summer months of our separation,
Will you be the scent of the first rains? I
asked.

I felt those biting cold months' torture,
When you ignored my wooing, I said.

Your stinging words rained with pain—
For a kind moment, I waited.

Against the strong winds of dry, stormy
months,
Did my feelings fail to reach your heart? I
wondered.

Like a fleeting autumn transition,
My hopes tossed from top to bottom; I felt.

Then came the days of fresh foliage and green
shoots—
A fleeting spring in my life, when I asked,
"Will you be my wife?"

Then came summer again—
The season of glorious sunshine; I rejoiced.

Followed by cold winters,
When only your love snowed, I enjoyed.

Your sweet tongue rained more words,
Now, only from the lips of my sweetheart. I
relished.

The winds of the past returned again,
Carrying my feelings in a circular motion. I
delighted.

The hues of autumn changed once more,
Transforming you into something more
beautiful than before! I stood amazed.

Spring bloomed again, a time for new gain—
Your love expressed without refrain, when I prayed, "Will you forever remain my sunshine?"

The seasons cycled time and again—
Yet, my all-season favorite, you remain. I realized.

Endless Longing of My Heart

Awaiting the sweet fragrance of your heart,
my love,
Those gentle whispers of your heart—I dote.

As hope mingles with sorrow, I yearn for your
sight,
Awaiting the healing touch to ease my pain,
O love—
That tender, mending touch of your embrace,
my dove.

Scorching is this wait, so long and filled with
tears, my dear,

A million eyes might picture my tears in your lipstick color.

Burning from this love, that consumes like a great hellfire,
I won't survive this dreaded drought that none admire.

Yet, in this love drought, I long for the rain of your care—
Pouring like rain, your sweet nectarine care, O love,
Remove this pain with your sweet embrace, my dove!

Having this body without its right soul, O dear,
I ask, what worth is a melody without right notes clear?

In deserted silence, I ponder the essence of
this fear—
Fearing you won't come, my wait far longer,
my dear,
I dread even my ashes won't get your
fragrance near!

Breathing life into life, make me alive, O my
soul,
Play this instrument with music that's pure
and whole!

Remembering the laughter and soft gentle
whispers, which were rare,
They've gone past swifter, like the untamed
winds on peaks higher.

As memories linger, so does my longing grow
stronger—
Watering the seed, nurturing this plant, the
love fruit we rear,
The sweet tales told only when the fragrant
flowers shower.

Longing for more, that grows thick and
strong, and stays forever,
Those moments came not, like the clock has
paused its endeavor.

In hoping amidst despair, my faith fails
never—
Waiting long, despite the pain I bear, for love
grows deeper,
For my tears and sighs—stamp of promises
and signs they declare!

Arriving here, my awaiting over, to end all my
despair,
Shine your grace to bloom my face in glowing
color!

Passing days failing to change me—will they
make you cheer?
Come, O my dear, my heart and
soul—heavens here witness bear!

From Lover to Love Eternal

Every journey begins only to meet its end,
The arrows that were shot meet their target.
Infatuations are not love, but are allowed in love;
What decides it is the moral compass.

Oh, my dear, I was too proud of my love.
A light illuminates objects, yet not itself.
Neither does a light illuminate another light.
Love thus reveals lovers, not the other way.

I met my last one, the final nail in love's coffin.
My destination has arrived; I bid adieu.
In the algebra of life, she will be my X,
A variable so valuable, yet weightless on its own.

Did she play her part in my journey?
Perhaps she knew not or knew too well.
I asked myself, "Is she happy without me?"
Perhaps yes, or perhaps no.

I asked, "Can she be happy without me?"
Yes, my answer. Perhaps the question is meaningless.
Will she journey with me, hand in hand?
Perhaps, or not; I can't tell now!

Why then bother to chase the happy state?
Can sugar be made sweeter further?
And her happiness by adding my love?
The answers hide within the questions.

What algebra did I resolve then?
The X was added to complete the sum.
It played its part and was needed no more.
The result now stands, eternal.

Oh, sincere students of my school of thought,
I once thought I was an eternal lover.
But my last love broke the record.
The narrow shell trapped me, broke,

And the being emerged, manifest instantly.
The lover is now love itself.
No light illuminates another light ever.
No love needs another love to trigger.

Objects need light; lovers need love.
Love, self-contained, needs no addition.
Be you my eternal love, not the eternal lover.
The shell broke loose, and the lover turned
into love.

The lover in me bid adieu gently,
Like mist dissolving in the morning sun.
The bees of a garden; the lovers of this Earth.
The honey of flowers; the love manifest in lovers.

The eternal lover no more, now eternal love manifests.
An X by itself is an unsolvable equation,
Yet without X, no solution exists.
Glory be to that X; now, I am that eternal love.

My problem solved, may you remain my eternal love.
No more two, the lover and loved; just one eternal love.

Eastern Blue Birds in Love Duet

Our bright plumage glows as we age,
Our love of the heart flows as we engage.
The time that tells tales of our times,
Witnesses our journey, in life's rhymes.

The nature stands a witness to our hearts,
Reflecting our feelings in its gentle winds.
Our hearts beat as one, in love's sweet song,
Echoing through time, where we all belong.

Genre V: Philosophy & Philosophers

The Four Divine Yogis

Karma Yogi

Mastered the art of labor's grace,
Through pleasure and pain, growing at steady pace.
Treat desire and anger as whispers of doubt,
Crafting each task as a work of the heart.

Bhakti Yogi

Master of the art of love's embrace,
In joy or sorrow, remains in sacred space.
Desire and anger dissolve in offerings made,
Blossoms in prayer and devotion's shade.

Raja Yogi

Master of the art of staying calm,
Remains a still lake when emotions storm.
Desire and anger, two fleeting shadows,
Dissolved in tranquil heart's fine meadows.

Jnana Yogi

Master of the art of balance, equipoise,
Sees pleasure and pain as passing experiences.
Desire and anger, clouds that drift away,
Illuminated always in wisdom's ray.

Krishna, The Self-Revealing Truth

Truth alone reveals itself,
Unaided and unprovoked.

Does light require another light
To illuminate the world?
It shines, and all is revealed,
Yet nothing reveals the light itself.

What sweetness can enhance sugar's taste?
What glory can elevate Krishna's state?

Krishna dwelled in Shivoham Shivoham,
A state of absolute solitude,
Where no second exists, no killer or slain,
Free from body, mind, and ego's chains.

Krishna declared himself unborn,
Not from madness, but truth profound.
He spoke reality, not philosophy's game,
For truth alone exists, philosophy is but a
name.

We adore the fleeting, fragile, and false in all,
Misnaming truth, which time cannot enthrall.
Truth is not a thing, but self-existent, whole,
The source of all, where appearances unfurl.

The permanent amidst change, absolute
freedom's core,
That alone is truth, forever revealing more.

Swami Vivekananda

A majestic soul, the power of thousand suns,
A hero's heart, which oozes kindness and
grace.
A thundering voice with musical notes,
Inspired talks, awakening a million souls.

A saffron robe, rich in philosophy fine,
Manliness manifest, a monk leonine.
A practical life, a world teacher true,
Created an order of monks, and souls set free.

A clarion call, to a nation imprisoned,
Arise, awake, and stop not till the goal is
reached.
A heartfelt word, outpoured with faith,
Expansion is life, contraction is death.

A Tribute to Adi Shankara

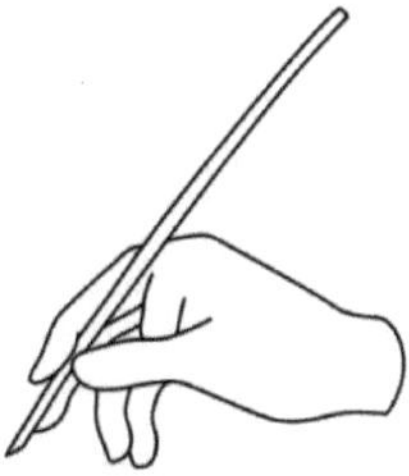

A bright young boy of eight years old,
Walked a long way in search of truth.
Met a man seated in meditation deep,
A sage whose wisdom was truly ripe.

Lived inside a cave in Narmada's bank great,
His soul realized in the cave of his own heart.
Questioned the young boy, "Who are you?"
Promptly replied the boy, "Self alone, all are."

Impressed, the sage initiated him as a monk,
Beginning a new age of revolutionary work.
To win back scholars, to set the record straight,
To reclaim the glorious Vedic life, set right.

Started four centers to keep the tradition alive,
Began in right earnest for scriptures to thrive.
An order of monks who carry his teachings in life,
To show to this world how to be free from inner strife.

Authored many hymns, oozing heartfelt devotion,
Commented on texts with standard explanation.
Wrote newer scriptures for easy comprehension,
Revived everything that remains as today's Hindu religion.

Time is Short, Abide in Love

No matter how majestic, how mighty, how grand,
The greatest lion will eventually meet a miserable end.
That's nature's cruel design.

At their peak, they reign, ruling with fierce might,
Chasing, catching, devouring, and leaving scraps for the night.
But time is a thief, stealing strength and prime,
Leaving the old lion weak, vulnerable, and blind.

It roams and roars, a shadow of its former
self,
Until luck runs out filling fate's cruel gulf.
Cornered by hyenas, nibbled, and eaten alive,
No mercy, no quarter, a gruesome, agonizing
strive.

Life is short, power fleeting, beauty lost with
time,
I've seen it in lions, in aging humans, in
corporate primes.
The mighty men and other powerful few,
Who ruled with iron fists, humiliated, and
broke through.

But their exits were miserable, their falls from
grace,
A reminder that everyone will meet their
vulnerable place.
So let us be humble, help the weak, the sick,
and the frail,
For we will all leave the stage, our final
curtain call.

Never forget, our time is limited, our strength
will wane,
And when we're gone, our legacy will remain.
So let kindness, compassion, and empathy be
our guide,
For in the end, it's not power, but love that
will endure.

The Traveler from the Void

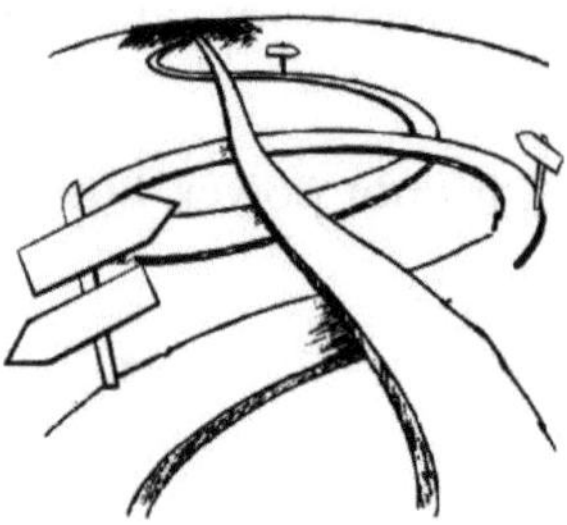

O men of this planet, come behold the stage well set.
This magic to unfold, a tale to be told, your lives reset.
I introduce to you a traveler from a No Land and Beyond,
Where the boundaries of reality fade into an unreal, volatile strand.

A No Land of people, having no bodies, no faces,
With a king, the ruler, with subjects from no races.
His reigns supreme from when there was no time,

With his subjects dead before they're born in time.

He wove a magical wand to end all beginnings and ends.
A fairyland emerged with no space, boundaries of no lines.
He got bored, and hence, laws of no rules alone gain,
Followed by chaotic orders and pleasures made of many pain.

All his no subjects of no faces, now all subjected to numerous tortures,
Put into prisons with no gates, to feel the fire made of chilly ices.
Ages thus passed, with No Time about to end,
Generations emerged and died, in space that never remained.

Until a subject arose, in whom clear wisdom rose,
The wise one proclaimed, "O my dear brethren and sistren, arise!

Hear my words of silence, with your hearts in reticence.
There was no beginning, from the beginning since,
And there is no end for you to hit an end in silence."

Neither was a king ever, nor any subjects that suffered,
Neither any events happened, nor any stories to unfold.
Nothing was created, never anything destroyed,
Nobody ever laughed, and none here cried.

In this No Land and No Space, neither you nor I have a face,
That which is alone here remains– better realize only this.
O men of this planet, come behold this magic to unfurl,
I introduce you to a journey that you never travelled to revel.

Crossing the sea made of no atoms, with
waves made of empty storms,
In a boat made of no matter, with its oars
made of silent stems,
To reach the shores, where truth awaits, and
wisdom restores,
Where alone there is a true shine, with light
from a sun fireless.

Burns bright with no fuel stain, removing all
your darkness vain,
O men of this planet, come behold this magic
without refrain.
Follow me into the realm of realms, where the
One Truth affirms,
And discover the secrets that lie beyond all
forms and regrets.

Genre VI: Humor

Ode to a Sniffly Gal Pal

How's your sneezy cold faring today?
Is it intensifying or subsiding by the day?

How's your sniffly health now?
Recovering fast, I hope, and not slow.

How much quicker do your days move on?
Unlike waves' ups and troughs, you may glide along.

How do your happiness levels measure?
Is it fuller, making your days brighter?

How's your lung's respiration?
Is it playing its own music, in tune?

How does it feel to breathe the air?
Does your nose still flow like a river?

Do you feel a butterfly frequently alight?
And wake up with loud roars in the night?

One problem, many questions, I know—
May all those questions have one answer:
Get well soon; healthier than ever!
Awaiting to hear you're feeling stronger!

The Great Diet Disaster

Hilarious History

I planned it for my diabetic Dad.
Traditional food was all he ever had.
Decided to test on me for a bit,
To ensure it worked and taste would fit.
In all earnest, we did a lab test for markers,
With Diabetologist and Nutritionist
explainers.

Tempting Trial

A tempting trial, I thought, was key.
Signed up with hopes for a healthy spree.
Day one seemed fine, a promising start.
By day five, I felt light and bright.

With the trial plan, things looked straight—
Less sleep needed; my spirits took flight.

Social Reactions

Though I felt somewhat fine,
My colleagues saw this light design,
Inquiring if my hunger had grown thin?
With fancy boxes, but little food within.
Some friends with curiosity bubbling,
Eager to see the disaster awaiting.

The Progression

My Dad refused, having set in his ways.
Challenging myself, I entered this new race.
Embracing the plan that had just began,
Listening to the measurements complain,
From Mom's motherly unbearable pain,
Me justifying the weight loss gain.

Inquiry Anecdotes

Eager inquiries in my office and acquaints:
“Can I crave for more, or stay in restraint?”
Some wanted more details about the
constraint,
Others, reasoning why they’d refrain.
Many making sweet, friendly remarks to join,
Asking details with an intent to learn.

Forsaken Goal

Backed by the science, precise and tight,
My palate turned as cold as winter night.
Midway, my grit faltered, letting in miseries.
I called it quits with gleeful, broken vows.

An Autobiography

A new routine, they said, I’d thrive,
But soon discovered I’d barely survive.
Measured portions, devoid of flair—
Every bite, a culinary nightmare.

Dreaded Woe

Then came the dreaded brinjal, my childhood foe,
Almost every meal, it made its show.
As fuel to the fire, a few more in the row,
My taste buds rebelled—this culinary woe.

Gastronomic Lament

From bland to boring, my tongue took a toll,
My quest for flavor, a forsaken goal.
Pleading requests for alternative equivalents
Were ignored, as recipes came from gourmet cuisines.

Broken Vow

As my woes began to grow with counting days,
An occasional delivery missing and delays,
Tested my patience, which wore thin smiles.
Midway, my grit weakened, bringing miseries.
I called it quits with gleeful, broken vows.

Post-mortem Pangs

After applying for the splitting divorce,
The company wanted to hear my unheard
voice.
With all ending on the right note, mutual—
A hilarious twist to my dietary tales:
A funny saga of healthy, unsavory meals,
My zest for losing weight, queued in
unfulfilled ideals.

The Flowery Quarrel: Unity in Variety

Pink Flower

I am the first of the season, this year.
The firstborn of my kind, you see.
I lead the way like great leaders do—
Unique, I stand; there's none to compare.

Yellow Flower

I thrive among my brethren here,
Not born alone, but in harmony.
I revel in company, as we all do,
My claim to uniqueness is not unfair.

Pink Flower

Not everyone leads the way, it's true,
I precede the season, proud and bright.
Wading and fading? I know not here—
Bold and brilliant, I stand glorious.

Yellow Flower

Leading needs someone following you,
I raise the season's glory with delight.
Multiplying many colors, so rare—
In a crowd of flowers, my presence
mysterious.

White Flower

What's this quarrel about, I wonder aloud?
In the spectrum of flowers, isn't each one
unique?
Though I've no rosy hue, I'm white and pure—
Together we bloom in joyous cheer!

Pink Flower

Oh, sweet white flower, you've color of cloud,
For we flaunt our colors; are you in a pique?
We get the thrill to lead with a flare.
Join us in the banter ring, if you dare!

Yellow Flower

Tease not the white bloom; it brings us delight,
In its gentle presence, we get the contrast right.
I respect its purpose; as a team we all blend—
In this vibrant garden, each other we befriend.

White Flower

This playful banter truly warms my heart,
In this game of flowery colors, I, too, take part.
Though I shine white and pure, my pedigree I lend,

In the harmony of flowers, I have my own blend.

Pink Flower

Welcome, whitey, to this game of throne,
We all together adore this mountain crown.
This friendly quarrel is meant to teach mankind—
None greater and nobody smaller, so be kind.

Yellow Flower

Well said, my pinky friend, we all are one.
Yellow or Pink, we all love adoration.
Our whitey friend is never left behind.
Playfully we told, O men, be more kind!

White Flower

In the midst of colors, we stand serene,
A canvas of peace in this vibrant scene.
We all speak of peaceful strides—
In unity, I find beauty and pride.

Together (All Flowers)

Let's not wage wars to prove great or small.
Each of us shines in our roles, standing tall.
In this vivid creation, unity is our song.
Together we bloom, and we get along!

Genre VII: Personal Reflections

Icy Whispers of Himalayas

Through glens and dales, my waters flow,
Through valleys and hills, where pilgrims go.
Though you seek to find my source,
My courses give joy, never remorse.

Through glens and dales, behold my trails,
Through valleys and hills, I weave my tales.
Though you seek to find my source,
My depths conceal a hidden resource.

Through glens and dales, I glide with grace,
Through valleys and plains, I carve my trace.
Though you seek to find my source,
My heart lies in icy glaciers.

Through glens and dales, my icy tales,
Through valleys and hills, my melting grace.
Though you seek to find my source,
I heal the world with gentle cures.

Through glens and dales, blow mighty gales,
Through valleys and hills, they sing solace.
Though you seek to find my source,
My ways and sways, they create rivers.

Through glens and dales, I feed the rivers,
Through valleys and plains, with my great
prowess.
Though you seek to find my source,
My endless and power nurtures and grows.

Fleeting Moments

Scene 1

In my long, sleepless nights in bed,
Trying to catch a dream ahead.
Sweet and sour memories vying—
Lyrical notes set my heart flying.

A strong and sensational ride,
No desire to open my eyes wide.
A journey with my thought mermaids,
Like mist dissolving when the sun invades.

Scene 2

Roaming high on open terraces,
No clear aim awakens my senses.
To distant sounds, my soul ignites,
Thoughts flood, like sudden cloudbursts in heights.

My stories have no end nearer;
Waking state spent as a dreamer.
Pictures and words come together;
Forgotten now—life's grown busier.

Scene 3

Trekking up on dizzy high peaks,
Lost away from the noisy buzz,
Ruminating—nice surroundings.
With feet on roll, spirit spinning fantasies.

Spotting random patterns galore,
All life lessons not to deplore.
Rested, grasping a long breath—
My weary mind lost a hundred poems' worth.

Scene 4

Riding back home, driving my way,
Detaching from the office away.
Setting my sights, crisscrossing roads,
Past pulsing motors that surge and go.

From honks and buzzes, mind detaches,
Choosing a million dreamy tracks,
Weaving interesting stories to match,
Profuse dreams diffuse, at home's reach.

Majestic Climbs and Sacred Trails

As I Begin in All Earnest...

I've waited long with tightly held breaths,
To view the misty, towering peaks.
Ready to craft my mystic tales,
Of whispers drawn from mountain delights.

Tracing through the winding path,
Treading a serpentine walk.
Leaving my old self far behind.

Climbing up and down the steeper slopes,
Like children on the see-saw boards,
I am the phoenix, from ashes reborn.

Morphing scenes are evolving clouds—
Collections woven from golden threads,
I embrace eachr new, constant challenge.

Beneath the sky, a vast canvas,
Reflects a spectrum of emotions bright,
In silent moments, my plans take flight.

As whispers of nature guide my path...

Verdant valleys, where my heart delights,
The journey carries me to childhood days,
Finding solace in a warm embrace.

A vivid spread of blooming flowers,
Painting scenes in myriad hues.
Scents of my beloved my nose invokes.

Lovely spires from ages past,
Legends from stories come alive,
From the days of bedtime story books.

Low and tall peaks in multitudes,
Teaching lessons about attitudes,
Sketching outcomes of life's endeavors.

As the sacred trail grows intriguing...

Each spire with timeless tales,
Portraying legends of highs and lows,
After great hard work come victories.

Majestic heights, a pure wonder,
Great heroes, humble and unafraid,
Never give up when facing obstructions.

Clouds kissing them with soft whispers,
Like the noble humans get praises,
My sweetheart whispers, her face in my
palms.

Snow-clad cheeks spark gentle smiles—
Sacred bonds, nature unwinds,
Mirroring my heart's blushes.

The sacred summit made me ponder,
The journey's end, where life begins.
With renewed vows for untried trails,
My soul uplifts in these sacred heights.

Reflections of Yearning

Feeling the first touch of rain,
Smelling petrichor's sweet scent—
A quiet promise of new beginnings.
Rustling leaves of big trees in the evenings,
Songs of early birds perched in fields.

Shining light at ten in cold seasons,
Parrots dart toward dense branches—
Their shrill squawks piercing through
evenings.
Shrill calls of blue peacocks' echo
As I hike up the quiet hills,
Monkeys in wild thickets begin their trills.

The supple touch of infants' fingers,
Their tender smiles and innocent thrills.
Stories spill from spongy lips—
Half-spoken words of baby darlings,
Echoing pure love all around us.

A gentle kiss on Mother's cheek,
The warmth of her lap, a quiet refuge.
Seeking her gentle arms, sleeping on soft
bosom,
Her gentle caress, a silent embrace—
A bond so pure, where love takes roots.

Licking the last of tasty remnants,
Walking beside the moving train,
Half-closed door, a friend departing,
Not letting go of love's hand,
Though not ready to say goodbye.

Closing my eyes from behind,
Of an unsuspecting friend,
Springing forth a sweet surprise,
Like an unexpected guest,
Sharing those pleasant experiences.

Unspoken love between sweethearts,
An unbroken vow lingers in silence—
Unending walks and unhurried talks,
With good friends on lonely paths,
A fulfilling feeling so divine.

A fleeting moment as my eyes meet hers—
Heart beats in harmony when the beloved is
near.
We sat in silence, which was eloquence,
Doing nothing, and yet everything,
A transient life, so fleeting and yearning.

Delicate touch of gentle breeze,
Subtle hints from nature surround,
Noises of leaves in a quiet forest,
Gleaming sun rays through trees at rest,
Each moment a whisper of what could be.

A distant voice fades in stillness,
Sight fixed on the open sky the earth touches,
Sparking thoughts vying to rush out,
Of untold stories that suddenly sprout,
A pure drifting allure.

A serene, mystic mountain,
A scene that quietly emerges,
On many journeys and my wanderings,
As if the earth was up and tilting,
Musings of poetry, inspiring more.

Unpresence

The stage is set, butterflies dance within,
A cart of thoughts, where secrets and dreams spin.
Shadows entwine with radiant, showy light,
Purple and orange flowers bloom, a wondrous sight.

Do rays of hope cleave through life's darkest veil?
Will dreams remain, and life's essence never falter or fail?
Are there shores waiting, for my heart to freely roam?
Or have I set up shop, in a place where none call it home?

Golden Elixir

Honey, ginger, lemon— each one is divine.
Mix them well, and shake and swivel.
On an empty stomach, sip it full and fine,
To summon good health, to glow and shine.

As morning sunbeams dance upon your face,
This golden elixir brings a warm, healthy
pace.
It soothes the throat, and calms the soul,
A refreshing start, to make your heart feel
whole.

Train journey

Train, a journey—
Chugging along with so many.

Choo, hoo-hoo, toot—
Noise of the engine beneath the foot.

Clickety-clack, roar, rumble—
Wheels on the track, their strength humble.

Phewoo, hoo, weet-weet—
Whistles that alarm are not so sweet.

Short or long, twisted and straight—
I ride along, with it on my journey flight.

River in a drop

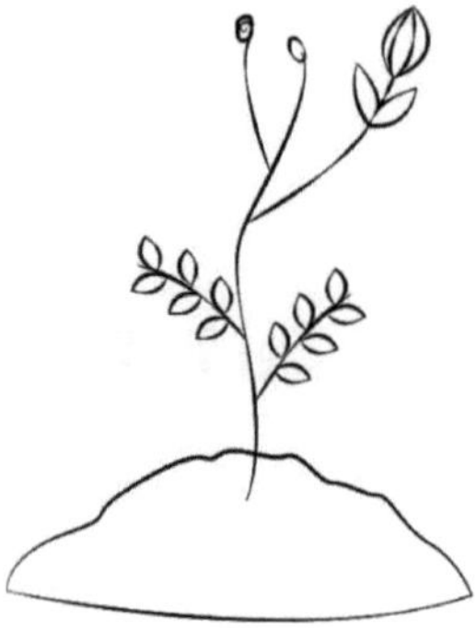

A drop of water,
  A leaf that gently holds.
A leaf on a twig,
  A branch that molds.
A tiny river flows,
  A microcosmic ocean wide,
All set in motion,
  A moment frozen in time.

Time is a Timeless Cycle

A clock shows the time,
Repeats countless times,
Marking moments lost,
As its hands move past.

Its steady ticking sound,
A rhythmic pulse that resounds,
Through hours, days, and years,
Passing through seconds that wear.

A clock shows the time,
Repeats countless times,
Birth or death that counts,
Between its one to twelve accounts.

The time is cyclical,
A truth within its circle,
It ends where it begins,
Hence, neither ends nor begins.

A book rack, soul's comfort zone

Stack of books,
Of tales and poems,
Stacked on racks,
Untouched by crooks.

As the pages turn,
With lessons to discern,
In it, my future glories await,
To awake with might.

The knowledge sparks,
Marked with many bookmarks,
Books are friends,
For the one who befriends.

Books that sleep,
Feeds the worms that creep,
Eyes that read,
Gain wisdom deep.

Knowledge from books,
Offers new perspectives,
Stories from books,
Brings new life lessons.

For the learned men,
Books are an inspiration.
For the seeking men,
Books are a comfort zone.

For eternal times,
Books do knowledge transfers.
In this knowledge space,
My soul ever finds its solace.

More, if it is shared

If only money grew on a plant;
Everyone might have been a farmer.
Just sunshine and wealth —oh, what bliss!
No more 9-to-5, no one stressed out,
No more bills to pay, no further debt.
Just harvest your cash and take a rest.

But alas, money doesn't grow on trees,
So, we trade our time for currency,
Sweating and toiling without mercies.
Yet, what if we cultivated kindness instead?
Might our hearts grow richer, and our souls
be fed?
Would there be abundance if everything were
shared?

A Farewell to a Friend and Colleague

Your laughter brightened days both near and far,
Though brief your stay, deep impressions that you made.
I've a promise to keep if we should part ever,
To capture your essence in poetical art portrayed.

Your vibrant presence, simple and unafraid,
We'll miss your warmth and tales to be told.
Your wit and charm, our moments glorified—
How shall we talk and banter, is it in future's hold?

Our promised profound talks remain
unfulfilled forever;
The details you claimed, though lost, were
clever.
Those amusing quirks and stories brought
more cheer—
Who'll relish my special dishes, anymore here?

Good be your smiles, good be your coffee's
taste,
Good be your luck, and may you find
Heaven's grace.

Birthdays: Life Unfolds to Grow

As birthdays come and go, years of life unfold and grow.
As we grow in age, wisdom's pages begin t to show.
As life's experiences gather in, our hearts with joy hope spin.

As birthdays come and go, years of life unfold and grow.
What's yet to come keeps hopes alive, shaping life's promises to thrive.
The days spent learning, to grow strong and ever-shining.

As birthdays come and go, years of life quietly show.
A flower blooms that bears fruits sweet,
actions may bear results to greet.
As you grow older daily, your life's lessons unfold readily.

As birthdays come and go, years of life unfold and grow.
Lessons learned, and wisdom gained, too;
your strengths and merits shine through.
As the morning sun rises high, self-awareness arises in your mind's eye.

As birthdays come and go, years of life unfold their glow.
As your new birthday and year unfold, may you shine like metal gold.
May your heart's purpose take root deep, and all your problems forever go to sleep.

Birthdays: Transience Revealed

As birthdays come and go, years of life quietly fade.
As we age, youth is forever lost in dim shade.
As old age creeps in, more weaknesses are displayed.

As birthdays come and go, years of life quietly fade.
What's gone is gone, and what arrives will eventually decay.
All that was learned will alone grow and stay.

As birthdays come and go, years of life quietly fade.
A flower blooms only to bear fruit anyway.
All learning must mature into wisdom each day.

As birthdays come and go, years of life quietly fade.
Let your flaws and merits be symbolically shed.
Let the wisdom of self-awareness dawn within you.

As birthdays come and go, years of life quietly fade.
Here's my wish as your new birthday and year unfold:
May your heart's purpose take root, and your true self be revealed.

Time's Enigma

Time is lost when it has passed.
Time remains ungrasped, even when present.
Deep questions linger as we exist;
How can we conceive if it is grasped or not?

Time's Testament

This and that of all that's past,
Names of ancient civilizations vast,
Buried deep, their remnants unearthed at last.
Their glories swept in tides of time, simply
aghast!

Millennia and eons have simply gone past.
For the past and future have all lost
In the firmament of nature's motion so fast.
Time alone stood as the testament at last.

Waves of events that swept the shores at
most,
In the grip of time, all remain tales of the
past.
Moment to moment seemed like forever to
last,
Yet things and people remain a memorial
spot.

In the cycle of time, some patterns repeat at most,
Unfolding scenes after scenes that move too fast.
What arrived here only became things of the past,
Time alone stood as the testament at last.

Innocuous Moments

Occasional moments, innocuous jokes,
Long misunderstood silence.
Accidental instances, innocuous situations,
Unintended consequences.

A glance that lingers, a moment's mistake.
Eyes meet, and embarrassment awakens.
Unintended gazes, awkward silences part.
Misconnection's pain settles in the heart.

A message sent with good intent,
Misunderstood, its meaning bent.
Words conveyed, but context lost,
Misread, and the purpose crossed.

Shower's warm, the doorbell rings,
An awkward pause, with dripping things.
A hurried bite, a surprise guest,
Awkward sharing, or an uneasy test.

My name mentioned, context unclear.
Overheard, and hearts filled with fear.
A shadow falls, thought of a friend,
A stranger's face, an embarrassing stand.

A conversation hushed, with awkward theme,
Uninvited arrival, discomfort's extreme.
Invited to join, a group with gracious charm,
Conversation drifts, with topics that rain
alarm.

A day of fasting, a vow to uphold.
Unexpected guests, a dinner to unfold.
A visit to the place in an uneasy state,
A moral dilemma, at a difficult pace.

A question abrupt, with a challenge keen.
A simple answer given, draws laughter unseen.
A moment's pause, a sudden surprise.
A hasty recovery, with awkward, nervous guise.

Genre VIII: History & Events

A Nation's Struggle and Triumph

1 Echoes of Legacy

Our hearts are heavy with hope we long to await,
Yet our deeds turned riches into fate.

A nation on its journey to glory,
From station to station of tales and stories;

One moment of hope, another of gloom,
Waging battles to win, shine, and bloom;

From being the midnight's children
To seeing the broad daylight vision;

The loaded legacies of Kings and Sages,
The tales that carry lessons and messages.

The distant past echoes without voices,
As the far-distant future hope waves arises.

2 Beneath the weight of tyranny

The gloomy, cold, wintery, lasting nights,
The scorching, bright, summery, exhausting
fights.

Wave after wave of continued conquering
races,
Sigh! Alas! and breathless energy-shattering
grimaces.

Fighting and dying; fleeing was never the
choice;
Be at wit's end; turning back was not a choice.

Tyranny of unseen proportions;
Tyrants of unimaginable permutations.

Looting, killing, demolishing riches, lives, and
properties—

Fighting to no avail; our spirits left in frailties.

Any hopes left for this nation to rebirth?
The frail spirits reignited, a million times worth.

3 The Flame of Resistance

In the forms of Tantya Tope, Jansi Lakshmi, and so on,
To revive battles that forever will go on!

The battles outnumbered more than the times we lost.
The gloomy clouds showered rains of terror fast.

When million stomachs waited for a few morsels,
No riches to spend on buying bombshells.

There arose warriors of another kind,
Where battles fought with fates intertwined.

Calls given to militate and revolt to drive the
enemy out,
Came from secret societies run by some
minds, bright.

What pain is felt from just a scratch or push,
When tyrants rule and our spirits, they crush?

So, roamed, another type that held pistol
guns.
That killed one or two enemies here and there
at once;

Been pooh-poohed by the enemy in a trice,
They suffered a great setback as the price.

4 Awakening to Change

Then came the trio of Lal, Bal, and Pal,
To start afresh and to return tit for tat.

The money-minded needed a monetary loss,
So, the trio showed us to boycott the clothes.

There were people of different races and colors,
Called Hume, of political and Annie, of spiritual nature.

Self-governance to Indians said one,
Home rule is my goal, stated the other.

When everything fades and voices grow feeble;
Some arose as poets, for the spirit not to fumble.

So much high went up the spirits,
The tyrants only issued them jail tickets.

Then came another who found a novel method,
That gave millions a new leader to be trusted.

His novel ways and methods, simple speeches and actions—
Quite unknown to a war-torn world of frictions.

Events after events resulted in more
bloodshed,
As the plot thickened to unite the nation
possessed.

More men and women who arose to create
unrest,
Unfortunately, given religious or ideological
colors by the rest.

5 Global Impact and Indian National Army

Meanwhile, the world saw two mighty wars.
Wealth and power corrupt as much as
burning desires.

If everything is fair in love and war,
Is it unfair only to love and stop the war?

Colonization wore a new face with Hitler
joining the stage.
Hitler's mirror showed colonization's ugly
carnage!

Hitler brought sworn enemies together unite;
From the Pacific to the Atlantic all teamed up to fight.

Was Hitler a clever nature's plan child?
To show all colonizers' morals defiled.

Heroic Subhash had his staunch plan;
The son of the nation reached the Land of the Rising Sun.

He built a trained army of hope.
For more support, he added the Russian scope.

Attack is the best form of defense,
To remove this foreign, immoral offense.

While his army met with partial success,
His end came in a mysterious mess.

Before the end of the world, there's the end of the wars.
At the end of the wars with a conscience that deplores.

6 Resurgence of Rebellion

The roars growing louder by the day,
The rebellious spirits kept the enemies at bay.

The hunters now find themselves as prey,
All acts of greed must return one day.

Ah, the English! Will their cunningness diminish?
Yet again they put this nation in great anguish!

When swords meet swords and guns facing a cannon,
A fight till death and bravery are common.

The clever, new method of Ahimsa met,
Crafty ways of divide and rule are well set.

Driving the sword to cleave the heart,
To let you bleed ever in protest.

Cowards discovered newer tricks,
To give you more painful pricks.

Even the lord of time lost his count;
Countless times colonizers' brains grew stunted.

They created rifts to stay adrift;
Their divisive actions, incredibly swift.

7 Dawn of Independence

We made a tryst with our destiny, swift,
Finally, with a new perspective shift.

During the midnight hours, when the world fell asleep,
A new India of hopes took a bigger leap.

Hopes inherited by a billion hearts,
Successes celebrated with vermillion marks.

The longest struggle for freedom in history,
That spanned across generations, gave us victory.

8 Ode to Unity and Strength

No nation is superior to mine!
None more glorious in civilization.

Long live my motherland,
Live long, her struggle stories.
Long live my homeland,
Live long, her strides to glories!

Long live peace everywhere,
Live long and prosper She.
Long live all those who play very fair,
Live long, such clans with guarantee.

Long live my victory song,
Live long, those who sing it in unison.
Long live my nation strong,
Live long, they, in a love-bound unification!

Shivaji: A Tale of Valor

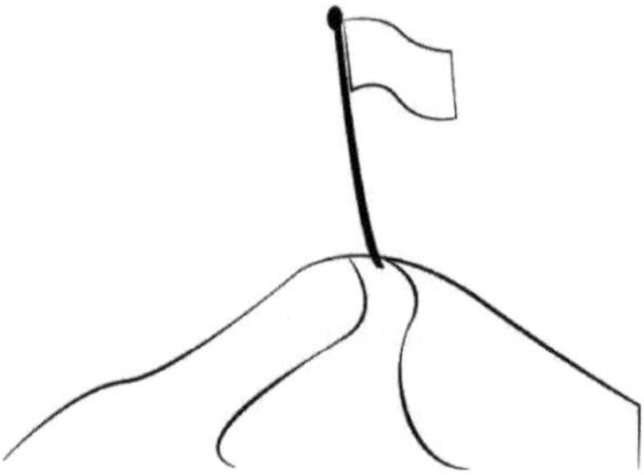

Signs emerge before the event;
Before ten, he sat on a horse mount,
With the cheers of mother confident,
To prove history in its unfoldment.

No dream's too far when the right seeds are sown.
In his young heart, proven greatness was shown.
Quests for conquests have been grown;
Even at sixteen, Fort Torana won.

A victorious first step among countless steps,
His every move became legendary leaps.
Raigad, Kondana, Sindhudurg followed next;
Sinhagad and Panhala too were brought.

Whoever said the sun rises in the east
Failed to notice it was born in India's west,
As Shivaji, the only great, with rays so
bright—
The baton of destiny was passed by divine
right.

One warrior inspiring unending legends,
Shaking the hearts of Deccan kings,
Shocking the mighty Mughal cantonments,
Facing challenges with heroic firmament.

From the lap of the Sahyadris
To the bed of coastal seas,
All enemies brought to their knees
With courageous fights on the battlefields.

Hiding and attacking with a new war
technique,
Mastering the art of a victorious streak.
His inspirational life for history to speak;
In forts and fields, his abilities wonder-struck.

Like seasoned chess masters,
Planning their moves well ahead,
This master of the battlefield
Made moves far ahead.

In the theater of war, a great conductor,
He orchestrated it as a maestro master.
Beating trumpets and blowing conches,
His army on ramparts forever marches.

Hiding like rats or biting like snakes,
Roaring like lions or mooing like cows,
Being in the field or starting some rumors—
All strategies he knew of warring tricks.

Winning over people with love and care,
Succeeding in his mighty endeavor,
Leading by living as an example—
A life that remained so simple.

Guiding his people with unwavering faith,
Standing very tall in turbulent times,
Sailing through rough seas not very smooth,
Anchoring the spirit of patriotic roots.

Finding solace in deep spiritual grace,
Rooted in culture's rich traditions,
Walking the path of dharmic embrace,
Creating an empire uniting all dominions.

Blessed child of Goddess Bhavani, he arose,
Living in the hearts of Marathas, he shines.
Igniting the soul of mother freedom, he
glows,
Beckoning with the calls of Swaraj, he
remains.

Jijabai: Mother of a Revolution

After centuries of wait—
A dream child was born.

What dream did the mother dream?
To unbind the slavery chain.
Nay, it wasn't a child like any other in the world.
All the majestic lions of the wild rolled into one brainchild.

The mother had an equal, none—
In grace, mettle, and determination.
She fed not the milk of her chest,
But only a great freedom quest to ignite.

Born of a noble warrior tribe,
That fought the invaders to survive,
Married at the age of eight
To a man leading a military might.

Inspired by a great sense of right (dharma),
Consumed by the self-ruling spirit (swaraj),
Learned in the Hindu religious rite,
Upholding the values of sacred merit.

She never chose to submit;
She only knew to commit.
She was born of flame to birth a fire,
Whose name in every heart became a fearless
sire.

Other mothers cultivate habits in children,
Jijabai cultivated Shivaji, a revolution.
When others lit lamps very bright,
She raised a beacon to glow in the darkest
night.

Heroes are not self-born;
They are only made by mothers.
Jija and Shiva were born—
As mother and son, made for each other.

Genre VIII: Celebrations

Festival of Illumination

The entire land bubbles in rejuvenation,
All her people cheer in new clothing fashion.
Joyous expressions fill them in and around,
In every little thing they do, life is found.

East, West, South, and North
People and culture give the festival significant worth.
On the thirteenth day of the dark fortnight,
Welcoming lords of wealth and health for delight.

Reminding us of the victory over Adharmic threat,
On the fourteenth instance, in the upcoming night.
Lighting lamps in houses and temples, warm and bright,
Illuminating the world with a glowing light.

Welcoming the bestower of wealth so abundant,
The goddess who favors those who are diligent,
To accept the worship, bless new ventures,
For communities engaged in trade and commerce.

Celebrating the nation's cherished hero ideal,
His glorious return, conquering a fearsome evil.
Celebrating the feats of a little boy in blue,
Lifting the mountain to defy the thunder god's angry brow.

Wielder of the wheel, killing the violent
perpetrator,
In a battle he fought, engaging his life
partner.
It triggered later these annual celebrations,
Making sweets at home, bursting plenty of
crackers.

On the new moon day of dark midnight,
When the goddess, whose color is the
blackest,
Many bow down, offering their reverence
best,
In the hours after the sun has set in the West.

Longing to wed the Lord, his consort did a
long penance
Following her lead, many spinsters keep
vigilance
Which goes on for eons, a practice in deep
devotion
Desiring to marry and tie the knot is a noble
tradition.

Jains and Buddhists too join this celebration
One remembers the day of the Tirthankar's illumination,
Others pay respects to Ashoka's transformation,
The Great, who set forth the peaceful mission.

Sikhs celebrate with a colorful presentation,
Remembering their Guru Har Gobind Singh,
Possessing youthful charm and great learning,
To mark the day of his freedom from Gwalior prison.

Siblings of two genders bond in affection,
Sisters praying for a healthy and fulfilling life for their brethren.
Hugging and wishing, feeding and sharing,
Nurturing the bond, with lamps for others' well-being.

Families and societies in joy affiliations,
Creating festive color, setting mood
vibrations.
Lighting many lamps, firing crackles and
sparkles,
A season of bonding removes afflictions.

Light bears immense importance,
Life is light, a glowing brilliance.
Light in darkness, where hope awakens,
Thus, all lights are held in high reverence.

Light to me is self-fulfillment,
A journey in the path of self-unfoldment.
Breaking inner enemies like crackers bursting,
Leading me into the great light,
soul-illuminating.

Festival of Lights, a splendid preparation,
Festival of Lights, a journey toward
transformation,
Festival of Lights, removing darker
countenance,
Festival of Lights, a festival of illumination!

Genre IX: Haiku series

Haiku series

Solitude Under Night Sky

Twinkling stars above,
Down came messages below,
My dreams now high soar.

Completeness

Late evening, moon rise;
The autumn season arrived;
My heart is fulfilled.

Hope Ignited

Vast expanse of sky;
Cold winds; dark clouds blown away;
I peeked at the stars.

Dawn of Wisdom

End of dark nighttime.
The horizon, orange bright.
Signs of wisdom rise.

Million Distant Hopes

Deep silent night skies.
Million lamps reaching my eyes.
Distant hopes await.

Divine

On high mountain tops,
Darkness thick, fog all around;
Peace, divine stillness.

Heart's revival

A long, dry summer.
Scent arising from the first drop.
Poem from my heart.

River of Life

River flows its path,
Human life, a journey long,
Ocean, God's embrace.

Soul Moon

The full moon shining,
The lake beneath, back smiling,
Mind reflects Soul, spirit.

Traditions

Formal, informal,
Shy fear yields to sacred respect,
Fixed, yet free, we stand.

New Year (Ver 1)

Calendar's turned page.
Numbers tell the story past;
More events await.

New Year (Ver 2)

Numbers flip, align.
Past shapes this moment arrives.
Promises unfold nigh.

Genre X: Children & Bedtime Stories

Starlit Dreams

A little child,
Hopes inside that softly glide,
Sat by my bedside.

Asking myriad questions,
Eyes in wonder, expressions—
Curiosity without obsessions.

What is a star?
How does it find its spark?
Why does it shine?

Bedtime stories spun,
Myths and science, all in one—
The child's mind is curiously drawn.

Started with a remark,
"I'm wonder-struck!
Our space travel, now we'll embark."

Sky's full o' splendor,
Crimson ball in slumber,
And brilliant moon yonder.

The ancient wisdom drawn from—
Greek and Egyptian myths,
Hindu and Phoenician gods,
Roman and Arab tales.

Learning of the challenges faced by—
Aryabhata and Bhaskara,
Al-Khwarizmi and Al-Battani, or
Galileo and Tycho Brahe.

Progression to the modern space treks:
Sputnik and Apollo's flight,
Rohini sparking ISRO's might,
The space stations that stay afloat.

Inspiring stories from the biographies of
Cosmonauts and Astronauts,
The astrophysicists and rocket scientists,
Who chart the stars and galaxies.

From ancient wisdom's first flight,
We now chart a newer cosmic height,
Creating vast stellar map chart,
A journey map from our bed spot.

Learning about polar stars,
Nebulae, birthplaces of stars—
We slowly slip into stellar dreams
And drift in the endless cosmic streams.

Moonlit Magical Glade

Once upon a time—
There lived a curious little child,
Who wandered into a dream-filled world,
Listening to adventure-filled stories,
Of friendships in enchanting forests.

On a lovely evening—
When the sky turned from copper to yellow,
A shimmering deer, with a fellow,
Both, with inquisitive eyes, progressed
Down one of their many mysterious trails.

The skyline turned grey—
As they strolled the path, the dark began to spar,
Stars lit up, twinkling bright and far,
Under moonlit pathways, they wandered,
And journeyed down uncharted ways.

The two deer rested a bit—
The narrator sensed the child's delight,
Then asked, "Do you love the forest tonight?"
The curiosity-filled little sweetheart,
Nodded her head, an answer clear and bright.

Stars began to twinkle brighter—
As they entered a magical glade,
A brief, gentle wind made the trees sway,
Lavender scents filled the air,
They found a gnarled tree stump at the
center.

The moon glowed with ethereal light—
They spotted an aged parrot with a beak,
She called to her guests with a squeak,
"Welcome, my wonder-filled new friends,
To the moonlit glade of beautiful wonders."

Emerald, the parrot, spoke—
As the winds blew with mystic might,
Bringing honeyed scents and sweet delight,
The branches showered flowers in bloom,
Turning deer coats to plumes of color.

The child sat upright, her hand on the
narrator's arm,
To clear away doubt, eyes sparkling with
charm,
She asked, "What is the deer's name, so
thrilling?"
"Jasper and Diamond," the narrator replied,
As the two deer ventured, their spirits started
swelling.

Seeking adventure, they asked Emerald,
"What secrets lie in the magical glade?"
Emerald, wise and full of grace,
Said, "Many treasures are yet to be found,
Follow me, and new paths will be laid."

She fluttered her wings and beckoned them
near,
They ventured deeper, hearts full of cheer,
Vines aglow among creepers abound,
That housed many sparkling fireflies,
Led them through the forest, magical and
profound.

Friendly creatures greeted their way—
Singing frogs in the nearby pond,
Dancing bees and beetles swarmed beyond,
Rabbits performing gymnastic feats,
In the enchanted glade, they found delight.

Rodents offered nectar and carrots to share,
Peafowls fluttered their feathers in the air,
Presenting an extraordinary musical choir,
The music-filled breeze made their spirits
soar,
Jasper and Diamond wondered for more.

"Are there more wishes to make?" they asked,
"Yes, for the brave and kind-hearted,"
As their eyes in excitement glowed,
The moon now shone on a tranquil pond,
A central island with treasures to find.

Step on the lily pad to reach—
The glowing island, quiet and serene,
Take care with each step, do not rush,
For the magic is all around you,
A place where dreams softly hush.

Upon the island, they felt at peace,
Enveloped by brilliant aura grace,
As if their wishes were granted with ease,
Then Emerald's joyous hoot rang clear,
"Hurrah! You've reached the lucky sphere!"

The treasure chest gleamed before them,
With labyrinths of vaults and artful hem,
A crystal ball inside with a magical gem,
Showing a forest surrounded by walls,
Offering wishes, to grant and to call.

Jasper went first—
"In the name of God, I thank Emerald and friends,
Who kept us entertained with so many treats.
Let all children hear more fun-filled stories,
And may I find more such magical glades."

Diamond, in turn—
"In the name of God, I thank all my new friends,
Whose blessed presence was pure in essence.
Let all narrators visit magical realms,
And may we be remembered in their tales."

Emerald, speaking with joy—
"In the name of God, I'm glad to find hearts so true,
Your journey through the glades was well worth the view.
May there be more such crystal-filled chests,
And may we find Jaspers and Diamonds in our quests."

The crystal ball glowed—
Jasper and Diamond, hearts full of grace,
Looked at the ball with quiet equipoise,
Wishing for children's dreams to take flight,
And for story-filled bedtimes to bring peace tonight.

As their wishes filled the air with delight,
Emerald gave one last joyous call,
The world began to fade, the stars dimmed light,
The child yawned softly, ready for the night.

"Goodnight, dear child," the narrator smiled,
"May your sweet dreams stream mile after mile."

Genre XI: Closure
Salutation

Title: Final Dedication

From the infinite, all is born,
In wholeness it exists, all unshaken and untorn.
Take or give, the whole still remains as it is,
In the circle of life, no losses, no gains.

May this collection reflect that truth,
Of boundless love, from birth to death.
In words, in dreams, in silent grace,
May we find the whole in every place.

Printed by Libri Plureos GmbH in Hamburg, Germany

9 789367 399118